David's Trust

Stronger Than Giants

Written By
Stephanie Tokpe

Illustrated By
Hadirat Yinka

Heart Like His Press

Printed in the United States of America
ISBN: 979-8-9998173-3-4
Published by Heart Like His Press
www.HeartLikeHisPress.com

DEDICATION

To my first godchild, David Kodjo,
Your eyes light up whenever we talk about the Bible, and watching you read God's Word on your own at such a young age has brought me deep joy. Being your godmother is one of my greatest blessings.

I also dedicate this book to all my nieces and nephews, who never hesitate to follow me to church every Sunday.

And to all the little hearts learning to trust God,

This story is for you!

Joshua 1:9 (NIV) "Be strong and courageous. Do not be afraid; do not be discouraged, for the Lord your God will be with you wherever you go."

David was the youngest of eight brothers.

He wasn't the tallest or the strongest, but he had something special,

a heart full of love for God.

David spent his days in the hills of Bethlehem, watching over his father's sheep.

He played music on his harp, sang songs of praise, and trusted God with all his heart.

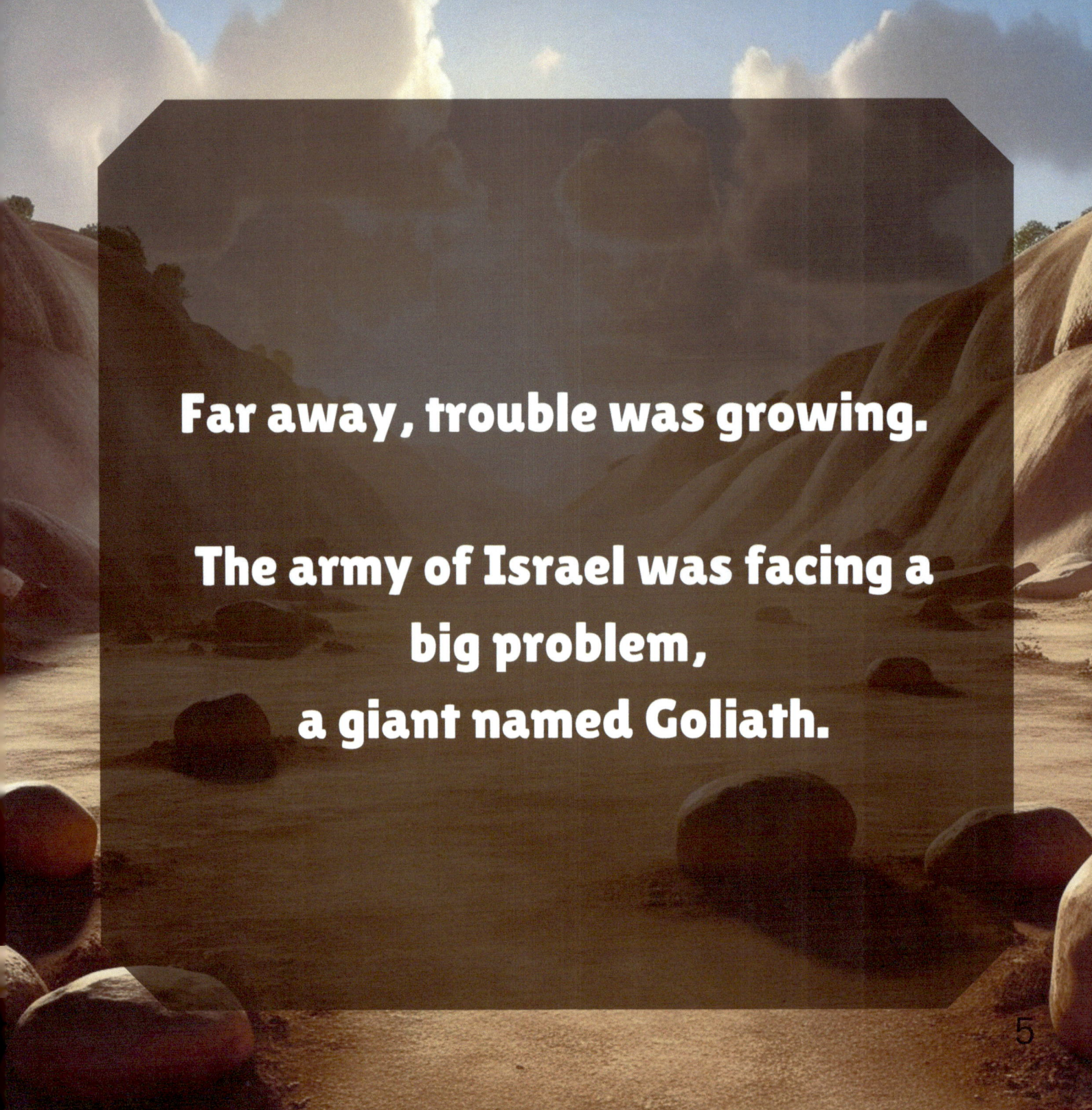

Far away, trouble was growing.

The army of Israel was facing a
big problem,
a giant named Goliath.

Goliath was tall and mean.
He wore heavy bronze armor and
shouted scary words across the
valley.

"Send me someone to fight me!"
he roared.

But the Israelites were afraid. No
one dared to step forward.

8

One day, David's father Jesse said,
"Take this food to your brothers at the battlefield."

So David packed bread and cheese and hurried to the army camp.

When he arrived, he heard a booming voice. It was Goliath, shouting again!
David saw the soldiers tremble in fear.

"Why is no one fighting him?" David asked.

"He's insulting the army of God!"

12

David stood before King Saul and said, "I'll fight the giant."

The king looked at him in surprise.

"You're just a boy," Saul said.

But David said, "I've fought lions and bears to protect my sheep. The Lord who saved me then will save me now!"

14

King Saul said,
"Go. And may the Lord be with you."

David didn't wear armor. He didn't carry a sword. Instead, he picked up five smooth stones and placed them in his shepherd's pouch.

15

With a sling in his hand and God in his heart, David stepped onto the battlefield.

Goliath laughed when he saw David.
"Am I a dog, that you come at me with sticks?"
he shouted.

18

But David stood firm. "You come with sword and spear," he said,

"but I come in the name of the Lord!"

"The battle belongs to God," David shouted,

"and today, He will help me win!"

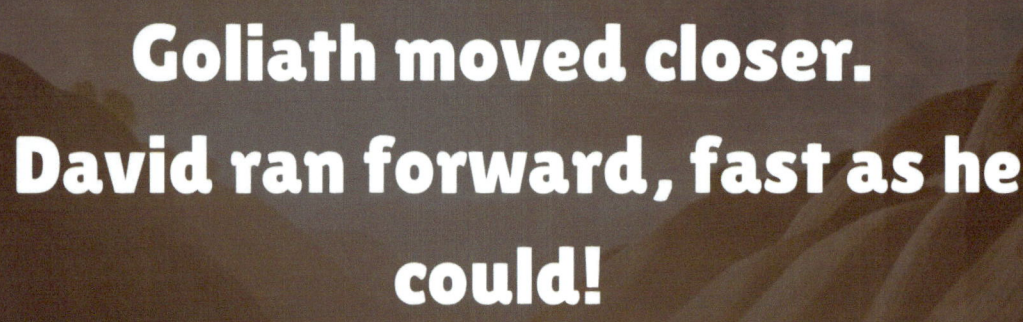

Goliath moved closer.
David ran forward, fast as he could!

He reached into his pouch, took out a stone, and swung his sling around and around...

WHISH—WHACK!

The stone flew through the air and hit Goliath right in the forehead.

BOOM!

The giant crashed to the ground!

24

With just a sling and a stone, David defeated the mighty warrior.

God had helped him, just like David believed He would!

Everyone watching was amazed.

"Who is this brave young man?" King Saul asked.

David smiled and said, "I am David, the son of Jesse of Bethlehem."

PARENT – CHILD ACTIVITY

David's giant was Goliath. But sometimes our giants look different. They might be worries, fears, or struggles at school or with friends.

👩‍👧 Talk Together:

– What is something you're struggling with right now?
– How can you be brave like David when facing it?
– How can trusting God help when things feel too big?

30

Helping Your Child Reflect

💡 *Use these hints to guide the conversation:*

1. Don't Let Size Define You: David was small and young, but God made him strong. Remind your child: "With God, you are more than enough."

2. Small Wins Prepare You for Big Victories: David's courage grew from protecting sheep from lions and bears. Encourage your child: even little choices such as being kind, telling the truth, are training for bigger challenges.

3. Be Yourself: Saul's armor didn't fit David. He used what worked for him, a sling and stones. Help your child see that God gave them unique gifts and personality. Their true self is their greatest strength.

4. Faith Over Fear: The army saw Goliath as too big, but David said, "The battle is the Lord's." Show your child how faith makes God bigger than any problem.

5. Your Victory Helps Others: When David defeated Goliath, the whole nation rejoiced. Remind your child that their courage can inspire and encourage friends, siblings, or classmates.

Every child will face giants.
But with faith, courage, and God's help,
even the smallest heart can win great victories
and inspire others to do the same.

BE
BRAVE
LIKE
DAVID !

34

HEART

LIKE HIS
PRESS

Stories that shape little hearts
to be like His.

www.ingramcontent.com/pod-product-compliance
Lightning Source LLC
Chambersburg PA
CBHW041615120626
46551CB00002B/450